Other Works by Tim Barker

My Jesus Journey

My Jesus Journey: Crescendo

My Jesus Journey: Glissando

My Jesus Journey: Rhapsody

Our Privilege of Joy

God's Revelation and Your Future

Truth, Love & Redemption: The Holy Spirit for Today

The Vision of Nehemiah: God's Plan for Righteous Living

End Times

At Your Feet

Anticipating the Return of Christ

Your Invitation to *Christ*

Your Invitation to *Christ*

Tim R. Barker, D. Min.

*Superintendent of the South Texas
District of the Assemblies of God*

YOUR INVITATION TO CHRIST, Barker, Tim.

1st ed.

Unless otherwise noted, Scriptures are taken from the NEW INTERNATIONAL VERSION (NIV): Scripture taken from THE HOLY BIBLE, NEW INTERNATIONAL VERSION ®. Copyright© 1973, 1978, 1984, 2011 by Biblica, Inc.™. Used by permission of Zondervan.

This book and its contents are wholly the creation and intellectual property of Tim Barker.

This book may not be reproduced in whole or in part, by electronic process or any other means, without written permission of the author.

ISBN: 978-1-7358529-5-9

Copyright © 2022 by Tim Barker

All Rights Reserved

Dedication

I'd like to dedicate this book to my predecessor as District Superintendent, Rev. Joseph P. Granberry.

Pastor Granberry served as Superintendent of the South Texas District Council from 2001-2011. He is a loving, compassionate leader who led our district through a series of challenges. His dedication and commitment positioned us to experience the goodness of God. His optimistic attitude frequently reminded us to "not let the devil lick the sweet off of your candy."

I'm honored to follow his superb leadership and grateful for the foundation he laid.

Tim R. Barker

Contents

Introduction i

REST 1

SEE 15

FOLLOW 29

DRINK 49

DINE 65

INHERIT 83

About Tim R. Barker 95

A Final Word 97

Additional Books by Tim R. Barker 99

Introduction

What's the secret to a better life?

How can we reach the pinnacle the world tells us we should strive for?

The truth is, we can't! No matter how high we reach, how many hours we work, all the connections we forge, success is always just one more handshake, one more paycheck, one more deal away!!

The only secret to a better life is no secret at all. It's through a relationship with Jesus Christ!!

How, you ask? What's the trick to this relationship that leads to a better life than we are able to achieve on our own?

No tricks. Jesus never tries to mislead us, pull the wool over our eyes, or does anything in secret.

In fact, He offers us an Invitation to the Greatest Show on Earth: Heaven. The world is getting ready as I write this. We've got a future you won't believe, and it's better than elephants, lions, and fancy moves on the high wire.

Our Invitation to Christ guarantees us six things. Once we accept Christ's invitation we can:

1. Rest. It's ours in the midst of whatever comes our way.
2. See. Our eyes are opened to the supernatural.
3. Follow. Christ is our only true leader.
4. Drink. The ambrosia of Jesus becomes ours.
5. Dine. We will find renewal in our fellowship with our Lord.
6. Inherit. The Kingdom will one day be ours. It's called Heaven.

Now you know, and since you've read this, you can never unknow. Salvation comes through Christ. God desires our presence, and we draw closer to Him through our Lord and Savior, Jesus.

Heaven is waiting. I want to be there.

Join me today, won't you?

We are a tired nation, living in both physical and soulish exhaustion, but the good news is that God has an invitation: "COME AND REST!"

— I —

REST

DO YOU find that you are often too tired and weary from life's struggles to simply survive?

Even with all our modern-day conveniences, I believe we could call ourselves the "TIRED GENERATION!" We are running around like crazy people from early morning to late at night because there are so many things to do and yet not enough time to get it all done. Not to very long ago, people would go to bed when the sun set, but now with electricity, we stay up late at night watching TV shows called "Late Night" and "Late Late Night" for those who really like to stay up late! And, we still have to get up early for work. No wonder we are all tired!

In many surveys, people say that they wish they had more free time or more time off. They wish they could just sit and do nothing for a while, maybe read a book, watch television or simply sleep in.

Even when we get time off, we fill it with so many things to do that often when we come back from vacations, we are just as tired, if not more so, than when we left! We need a vacation from our vacations!

Could it be that the greatest problem is not the tiredness of body but the tiredness of our tired souls; that we have grown tired as a nation over evil in our land, over corruption and terrorism left unchecked, over the constant themes of poverty and disease and brutality? If you're like me, we grow weary of the unchanging face of sin, of evildoers getting away with their deeds. We have become cynics about nearly everything from politics, to jobs, and even religion!

This is a serious issue. Because of our tiredness of soul, children grow up neglected or hurt from broken homes, parents try to fill their lives with business and extended work hours to make themselves believe they have something important to live for or to make more money ... and teens don't have direction in their lives as they don't see anything to live for except rampant materialism.

We are a tired nation, living in both physical and soulish exhaustion, but the good news is that God has an invitation: "COME AND REST!" God is quick to invite us to come to Him; He is the answer to our tiredness of soul! The Bible teaches us that there is a rest for the soul even when life gets hectic; this rest is deep and refreshing and satisfies!

Matthew 11:28 says to us:

"Come to me, all you who are weary and burdened, and I will give you rest."

The secret to finding the rest that every human soul longs for is found in these first three words of Jesus' invitation: *"Come to ME!"* Jesus doesn't mess around with truth and what each soul needs, He simply declares that if you are to find *"rest"* for your soul there is only one place to get it ... not just from Him but IN HIM! He identifies no other source for rest other than *"IN Him."*

The world tries to find this rest in so many other places:

- *They build big resort areas.*
- *They use sports events.*
- *They go on vacations.*
- *They seek out philosophies.*
- *They seek out strange and wild religions and meditation.*
- *They seek out the occult.*
- *They seek out pleasure from a variety of sins and immorality.*

Nothing in this world has provided the rest for the soul except Jesus!

The soul can find no rest in the things of this world, it can only be found in Christ! An eternal soul needs something eternal to rest in. If you are running around looking for relief from this world's burdens and trials, you won't find it in this world. If you are truly tired of running around trying to find rest for your heart and mind, look no further. Jesus is here for you now and is making an invitation for you to come NOW to Him for real rest!

Matthew 11:28b offers this encouragement:

"All you who are weary and burdened ..."

Well, that about covers everyone!!! *"... and I will give you rest!"* There is no question about what you receive when you come to Christ, IT IS REST! Just so you don't get the wrong idea, however, Christ is not offering a life without trials and difficulties, but He does offer security of the soul no matter how bad things get or how difficult things get! This word translated *"REST"* in Greek is *"anapausis"* not *"katapausis."* Thus it is better translated *"RELIEF"*... it is not therefore a life free from pain or struggle or sorrow, it is a security from being overwhelmed by life's struggles, and in this sense it is a rest from heaviness!

In Christ there is a security that cannot be found in this world. As Christians we are not crippled or crushed by events that come and go in our life. Even the most tragic of events cannot break our spirit when we abide in Christ. This is the security of Christ's offer of rest ... in Him we have purpose and in Him *"we know that all things work for our good!"* Even the most perplexing events in life that can never be explained or understood cannot rob us of the rest we find in Christ! In this world there is no rest like this!!!!

Just going to church and learning to recite the right prayers won't bring it either, **you must set your soul on Christ!**

Christ's offer here has no *"maybe"* in it; it is certain that if we trust in Christ, our soul finds rest! You do not have to go through life worn down in your heart; you can find a *"relief"* and peace in Christ. While things in this world offer a temporary peace or some physical rest, nothing will satisfy your soul except God!

Matthew 11:29 reveals Jesus' tender heart;

"Take my yoke upon you and learn from me, for I am gentle and humble in heart, and you will find rest for your souls."

Jesus now explains the secret to finding real rest in Him. It is to exchange the yoke the world puts on us and instead put on Christ's yoke! The secret to rest is not inactivity ... it is right activities! Jesus didn't say *"quit working"* ... He said to put on *"His yoke"* so we will head in the right direction, and when it gets tough, He can do the heavy work and pulling!

Jesus invites us to learn from Him. He was not inactive, but He sure wasn't overwhelmed either! He drew His strength and peace from His father, and we are to draw ours from Him! Jesus did not worry ... not once do we read that He was worried or anxious about anything! In fact, worry only makes matters worse; it is not good for us! This is why Jesus also said, *"Be anxious for nothing!"* Birds don't get up in the morning and worry about whether there will be enough worms that day! How many dogs do you know that have had nervous breakdowns?!!! My dog

Domino watched the news every night with me, and she never once fretted over life! Ever seen the animals in the forest call a meeting to see how they are all going to make it the next week?

We are called upon by Christ to *"learn from me."* How did He handle everyday life? He prayed and trusted His father for everything! He did whatever He could each day and did not fret over tomorrow. He focused His energy on relationships, not things. He looked each day for what He might give, not what he got! He valued spiritual realities far above the things of this world. He sought to forgive, to love, to be patient, to heal.

If we lived and patterned ourselves after Christ, our lives would be very restful!

Jesus clearly identifies the kind of rest He is speaking about: *"for you will find rest for your souls."* It is not a rest from activity or planning, or hard work! It is a rest for the soul amidst all the good and bad of life, all the activity and trials, the joy and the pain.

Jesus explains what He is like: *"I am gentle and humble in heart"* ... this is how we are to pattern ourselves. He is gentle in that He seeks to harm no one; He is not one to hurt or to condemn; His gentleness is demonstrated in how patient He is with sinners and saints who don't obey Him; and His patience is marvelous! His humility puts others ahead of self ... He did not come to be served, but to serve others. This is hardly the mentality of the world because it is spiritual in essence and thus the world does not grasp it! Rest cannot come if we don't pattern ourselves after Christ in these two ways! People who are demanding and angry or who act superior to others and so have a demanding spirit are some of the most frustrated and tired people on earth!

We cannot escape a YOKE – we WILL and must choose one! What are you yoked to – a career, a lifestyle, an organization – or Christ??? The only yoke that is not too heavy to bear is the one that is connected to Christ! If you want to find relief, it is spelled C – H – R – I – S – T! That's how you spell RELIEF! *(Remember the meaning of the Greek word for "rest" is "relief.")* Those that walk with God never lose their way; they can't when they are yoked to Him!

In these last days, the Bible says in Hebrews 12:26b:

> "Once more I will shake not only the earth but also the heavens."

The words *"once more"* indicate the removing of what can be shaken – that is, created things – so that what cannot be shaken may remain. *"Therefore, since we are receiving a kingdom that cannot be shaken, let us be thankful"* (v. 28a).

Do you know what is unshakeable to yoke yourself to? *"His yoke is easy, his burden is light!"*

He is unshakable and His kingdom endures!

We do have a choice, a light burden or a heavy one! Only the fool chooses the heavy one – so choose Christ. He invites you to *"COME AND REST!"*

Do you want real rest? It is available, why not

accept Christ's invitation?

There is a deeper rest than physical rest! You can be quite active and still find rest in Christ! People today are tired! There is an exhaustion of the soul that can only be refreshed IN Christ. Jesus' invitation is very clear, *"Come to me, all you who are weary and burdened, and I will give you rest!"*

How tired are you, and have you discovered God's invitation to come and find real rest? The invitation is a good one!

"COME AND SEE!" – come and see the real meaning to life. It is not found in a thing but in a person called Jesus Christ!

— 2 —

SEE

WHY DO people flock to all kinds of teachers and seminars? Why do people jump from one thing to another thing? They are all desperately searching for meaning and satisfaction in life!

One of the main reasons people commit suicide is that they cease to believe there is any reason for living anymore, that there is no meaning or purpose to life — so they quit, they give up.

The world is a battlefield today; the forces of darkness are competing for the souls of men and women, drawing them to meaningless existences while filling their lives with so much busyness that they have no satisfaction in anything – and to distract them from the real meaning in life.

With all the emptiness in this world, God shouts from the heavens and makes an invitation: *"COME AND SEE!"* – come and see the real meaning to life. It is not found in a thing but in a person called Jesus Christ!

The Bible teaches us that the only real meaning in life is found in a living relationship with God through Jesus Christ. We are invited by God to come and see this for ourselves by inviting Christ into our lives.

John 1:35-38 tells us:

"The next day John was there again with two of his disciples. When he saw Jesus passing by, he said, 'Look, the Lamb of God!' When the two disciples heard him say this, they followed Jesus. Turning around, Jesus saw them following and asked, 'What do you want?' They said, 'Rabbi' (which means 'Teacher'), 'where are you staying?'"

Andrew and John had become disciples of John the Baptist; they were interested in his call to a real life of service to God. They had felt a real need to know God and through following John the Baptist they had felt something tugging on their hearts. Fishing had not been enough for them. While it provided a means of living, it didn't provide satisfaction for their souls! This is still true today. People are always looking for that job or place that will satisfy the longing of the heart, but when they get them, they discover that ultimately these things still don't satisfy them long term. Though they certainly had enjoyed the ministry of John the Baptist, Andrew and John heard him say one day when Jesus was passing by that Jesus was the *"Lamb of God."* John the Baptist was not the answer, he was only the one who would point the way to the real answer. The real meaning in life was found in Jesus! When that day came, John the Baptist pointed them toward Jesus, the one who could meet their deepest needs and desire — the one to give them meaning!

They had wandered here and there in their life, and they were tired. They wanted the real thing, much as people wander today looking for meaning!

Both Andrew and John immediately left John the Baptist and began to follow Jesus ... but even here there is a hint that they didn't really understand what it was they were looking for or had found. Jesus turns around and asked them an interesting question: *"WHAT do you want?"* – NOT *"WHO do you want?"* This indicates that Jesus knew that they were seeking SOMETHING rather than SOMEONE to fill their need.

This is still the probing question for everyone: *"What are you looking for?"*

The answer is somewhat of a surprise, however, for satisfaction in life will never come from a THING. It will only come from a PERSON – THE PERSON OF JESUS CHRIST! Their response to Jesus' question indicated that they didn't understand who Jesus really was even though John the Baptist had clearly told them that Jesus was the *"Lamb of God"* – they still referred to Jesus simply as *"RABBI"* meaning *"Teacher."* They didn't see Him clearly at all! They saw Jesus in the way they saw John the Baptist, as just another teacher. Much of the world still sees Jesus this way.

Jesus could tell they were looking in the wrong place for their satisfaction, so He was about to share an important message with them.

Notice what Haggai says about people living in his day in Haggai 1:5-9:

"Now this is what the Lord Almighty says: 'Give careful thought to your ways. You have planted much, but harvested little. You eat, but never have enough. You drink, but never have your fill. You put on clothes, but are not warm. You earn wages, only to put them in a purse with holes in it.' This is what the Lord Almighty says: 'Give careful thought to your ways. Go up into the mountains and bring down timber and build my house, so that I may take pleasure in it and be honored,' says the Lord. 'You expected much, but see, it turned out to be little. What you brought home, I

blew away. Why?' declares the Lord Almighty. 'Because of my house, which remains a ruin, while each of you is busy with your own house.'"

The people at that time believed in God but their lives were busy with their own pursuits – God had little priority in their lives. (This is similar to today!) And yet, the more they worked for themselves, the emptier they felt; while they seemed to work hard for what they got, they ended up with feeling emptier and emptier. They had neglected God's house while building their own; they put God on the back burner in their lives and so were not gaining! This Old Testament passage is the parallel to the New Testament passage where it is written, *"Seek first the Kingdom of God and His righteousness and all these other things will be added unto you."*

Their answer to Jesus' question, *"What do you want,"* is, *"Where are you staying?"* They thought Jesus might give them a place of security, a place to teach them, a place to settle down. They were simply looking for a place to rest, but Jesus will show them something very different from what they might have thought they needed!

John 1:39a reveals the response of Christ:

"'Come,' he replied, 'and you will see.'"

So, they went and saw where He was staying, and they spent that day with Him. It was about four in the afternoon.

They had asked Jesus *"Where are you staying?"* and Jesus responds with *"Come and see!"* While they think they are heading off to some safe place to find security, perhaps a camp where Jesus will teach them the meaning of life, Jesus has in mind however to show them the real place of security! Their focus is the material realm; Jesus however has something very different in mind for them. Where will Jesus take us that will give us meaning and peace in our lives? Jesus' plan is to show them that security is not found in *"something"* but *"someone"* – namely HIM! Christ's offer is still good: *"COME AND SEE!"* – CHECK HIM OUT!

They must have been disappointed when they arrived at the place Jesus had invited them to *"come and see!"* – and what they discovered was only Jesus! There certainly wasn't anything spectacular about the accommodations Jesus took them to! How could a place like this offer satisfaction? Jesus begins to open their eyes to see that it is not a PLACE, but rather, it is a PERSON ... namely Jesus Himself!

If it was some PLACE or some PROGRAM they hoped to find, they had to have been disappointed!

Jesus later taught them in Luke 9:58:

"And Jesus said unto them, 'Foxes have holes, and birds of the air have nests; but the Son of man has no where to lay his head.'"

Jesus didn't put His trust in places. There is no place to lay down or settle down and find real peace, at least not on this planet! There is a better place, and the way to get there is through a person. It is Jesus Himself!

They needed to modify their understanding of security. It can't be found on this planet; it will only be experienced in Heaven – and the way there is only through Christ! This was a unique message; all other religions promise redemption only if you accomplish some level of success at doing enough good works! Jesus was making the path to security through Him – not through us! They spent the entire day with Jesus until four in the afternoon, and Jesus did show them the place … it was in Him!

John 1:40-42 reveals Andrew's revelation:

"Andrew, Simon Peter's brother, was one of the two who heard what John had said and who had followed Jesus. The first thing Andrew did was to find his brother Simon and tell him, 'We have found the Messiah' (that is, the Christ). And he brought him to Jesus. Jesus looked at him and said, 'You are Simon son of John. You will be called Cephas' (which, when translated, is Peter)."

Now that they had accepted Christ's invitation to

"COME AND SEE," they realized that Jesus was not just *"RABBI"* ... He was *MESSIAH!* Andrew could not keep this news to himself; he needed to go immediately and find his brother Simon to share this *"good news"* – the very meaning of the term *"Gospel!"* Jesus had honored His invitation; THEY HAD COME AND THEY HAD SEEN! Their understanding had been opened and their excitement started to pour out. This was too good to keep to themselves! They had found what they were looking for; finally, their search had come to an end. Now everything else in life would hold meaning. They could survive the worst of trials and experience the greatest of joys known. Their lives were now fulfilled in Christ, the Savior.

They had found something they could finally trust their lives to ... Jesus.

Now that they had found salvation in Christ, it became a passion for them to bring others to Christ! Andrew not only takes the message to his brother Simon Peter, he also leads him back to Jesus to SEE for himself! Andrew doesn't ask Peter to be like him, but to find Jesus and be like Him! This is the purpose of ministry – to bring others to Christ! Andrew couldn't offer his brother, Simon, a perfect brother, but he could offer him the perfect Savior!

It is not enough that we find satisfaction for our own souls, we must also look to share it with others! No matter how imperfect those others might be, they too need to find the meaning to life in Christ! When Simon came to Jesus, his life, too, was transformed. He was given a new name along with his new life, and he, too, found the greatest longing of his heart!

Andrew and John were looking for something special for their lives, for significance and meaning. Jesus invited them to *"come and see"* – to come and see what was really important in life. What they saw was different from what they expected at first, but Christ gave real meaning to their lives, and He still does today!

Have you accepted Jesus' invitation to *"come and see?"* The invitation is still valid and open today.

Only by throwing yourself and your priorities on the mercy seat of God can you find salvation! Jesus must become your priority and means to salvation!

— 3 —

FOLLOW

PUBLIC SURVEYS indicate that most people believe they are going to Heaven! The fact that most Americans believe they are going to Heaven caught the curiosity of a reporter from WMBI in Chicago. Walter Carlson decided to hit the streets with a microphone and ask people the next logical question: *"How does a person go to Heaven?"* For over half an hour in the city's Union Station, he asked this question, and these were the most common answers he got from people:

> *"Obey the Golden Rule"*
> *"Be good to your neighbor"*
> *"Go to Church"*

"Do good deeds"
"Pay your bills"

Few people got the right answer! God's invitation to *"Come Follow Me"* is known by most people, but most people are not listening to Christ's explanation on *how* they can come and truly follow Him.

These two passages of Scripture will teach us that many people are not willing to follow Jesus when they really understand what the invitation really means. Yet, to those willing to follow, the supernatural power of God is ready to flow through them!

Mark 10:17-31 gives us God's plan:

"As Jesus started on his way, a man ran up to him and fell on his knees before him. 'Good teacher,' he asked, 'what must I do to inherit eternal life?' 'Why do you call me good?' Jesus answered. 'No one is good—except God alone. You know the commandments: "You shall not murder, you shall not commit adultery, you shall not steal, you shall not give

false testimony, you shall not defraud, honor your father and mother.'"

"'Teacher,' he declared, 'all these I have kept since I was a boy.' Jesus looked at him and loved him. 'One thing you lack,' he said. 'Go, sell everything you have and give to the poor, and you will have treasure in heaven. Then come, follow me.'

"At this the man's face fell. He went away sad, because he had great wealth. Jesus looked around and said to his disciples, 'How hard it is for the rich to enter the kingdom of God!' The disciples were amazed at his words. But Jesus said again, 'Children, how hard it is to enter the kingdom of God! It is easier for a camel to go through the eye of a needle than for someone who is rich to enter the kingdom of God.'

"The disciples were even more amazed, and said to each other, 'Who then can be saved?' Jesus looked at them and said, 'With man this *is impossible, but not with God; all things are possible with God.' Then Peter spoke up, 'We have left everything to follow you!'*

"'Truly I tell you,' Jesus replied, 'no one who has left home or brothers or sisters or mother or father or children or fields for me and the gospel will fail to receive a hundred times as much in this present age: homes, brothers, sisters, mothers, children and fields – along with persecutions – and in the age to come eternal life. But many who are first will be last, and the last first.'"

We are introduced to a rich man who is anxious to see Jesus – *he comes running* – in order to find satisfaction for his soul. Matthew tells us this man was *"young."* Luke calls this young man a *"ruler."* Mark tells us he is *"rich."* This man had everything this world had to offer: power, money, and youth! Yet he comes running to Jesus ... it is obvious by his anxious attempt to get to Jesus that he was still missing something significant in his life; there is an emptiness to his existence that he cannot shake off nor fill from the stuff of this world. Not only did he run to Jesus, but when he got there, he immediately knelt down to Jesus in front of strangers on the road in public! He was quite impatient to talk to Jesus about his emptiness and appears to be willing to humble himself! It seems his desire to know how to be saved was sincere and strong! As a rich man, he was not used to waiting for things. Perhaps this explains his impatience, also. He was used to getting what he wanted right away!

It's apparent that in his mind, getting what he needed from Jesus was a simple matter of doing something. Notice his question: *"What MUST I DO to inherit eternal life?"* He assumes what most people today assume, that they can do something for God to let them into Heaven! His greeting of Jesus lacks understanding about Jesus' true nature, an issue Jesus will deal with first ... he simply addressed Jesus as *"good teacher."* If Jesus is simply perceived as just another man, another *"good teacher,"* then the whole idea of salvation becomes a man-oriented effort! This will have to be corrected first before Jesus can go on!

The Lord now addresses the issue of "who" He

really is by asking the man why he called Him *"good"* ... after all, only God can be called *"good!"* Jesus is not rejecting the idea that He is God here, in fact just the opposite. He is trying to make the man realize that this is exactly who He is ... God! The man was correct to call Him *"good"* because He is God, but did the man truly understand this? This was necessary before Jesus could explain how this man was to be saved. He needed to know Jesus is God and therefore to FOLLOW HIM!

With this issue settled, Jesus now asks him about his knowledge of God's Word and how well he has done living up to it. The man responds that he has kept the commandments of God from his childhood, yet he is still feeling empty. Why? It is interesting to note that Jesus does not challenge the accuracy of his statement that he had done all the right things, but this was exactly the barrier for this man ... his good works had given him a false sense of salvation. Yet, he still didn't have a living relationship with God! Jesus was opening this man's eyes to see that it wasn't just DOING something for God that saves, it is BEING something ... a follower of Christ that counts.

The man's priorities in life were his problem ... he had put *"doing"* above everything else. As a hard worker he had gained great wealth and power ... but not salvation! Jesus was about to challenge his priorities by asking him to do yet one thing more to prove how much he really wanted to find salvation. Obeying the Ten Commandments was not enough; he needed a relationship with God first!

Is this man's desire to find salvation greater than anything else? Jesus tests his priorities by asking him to *"go sell everything you have and give to the poor and you will have treasure in heaven, then come follow me."* After all, he did ask Jesus, *"What must I do to inherit eternal life?"* Is he as anxious to get salvation as he claims to be? This truly would test his true priorities! Jesus was offering to make him rich in another way, promising *"treasure in heaven."* This would go deeper than just outward obedience; this would strike at what was truly in this man's heart — what did he truly love the most!?

It was interesting that in the early part of verse 21, *"Jesus looked at him and loved him."* Here is a truly *"good man"* ... one who had obeyed the Ten Commandments but was realizing that things don't satisfy deeply. It was easy to love this man as he was really searching for meaning! The real issue was how deeply he wanted to find salvation; how much was his heart controlled by these other worldly loves!?

Tragically his response to Jesus' suggestion was deep depression; he became very sad, and in fact he walked away from God – thus revealing that he was not yet willing to give up his love for this world's stuff to get spiritual stuff! His love for earthly treasure was yet greater than his desire for heavenly treasure. His heart was too captivated by what this world had to offer. To change his priorities was too painful and costly after all, so he walked away from God – still a good man, but still a lost one!

This man's face fell at the price he would have to pay to make Jesus the top priority in his life! He was willing to live a good life, just not a godly one! This is the same stance many people choose today; they are ok with just being *"good"* – and they are willing to accept this over being *"godly."* This was just too high a price tag for the rich young ruler's wallet! Comfort of the soul took a second place to comfort of the wallet!

Jesus now explains how difficult it is for those whose priorities are placed on this world to come into the kingdom of God. The greater the passion for this world's stuff, the more difficult it is to have passion for the kingdom of God! If the rich man could have added Jesus to his wealth, he was willing, but to make Jesus more important than his wealth was going too far! The phrase here, *"How hard it is for the rich..."* can also be translated, *"How hard it is for those who have things to enter..."* indicating that it is not just hard for those with monetary wealth but anyone who places a greater priority on this world and what it offers! The rich man wanted salvation, but not at any cost! There are many people today who are taken with the idea of spiritual things, but they are not willing to pay any price for true spirituality! And, like this man, most of these people today are also good people!!!

The disciples were really blown away by these statements of Jesus. Their surprised reaction reflects the common notion of that day (and this!) that material blessings are a sign of God's approval on someone! If it is therefore hard for good rich people to be saved, then where did that leave them? How we envy those who have much of this world's stuff; we think they are happy and have God's blessings on them. Not only was this guy rich, but he obeyed the Ten Commandments ... and Jesus said he still was lost! No wonder in verse 26 they were said at this point to be *"astonished!"* Their whole concept of salvation was being challenged as well!

The disciples' confusion basically went like this: *"If rich people aren't proof of God's blessings and approval, and those who keep the commandments of God aren't proof either, then it is impossible for a man to be saved!"* That would mean a man could do nothing good enough to be saved! AND THIS WAS EXACTLY JESUS' POINT! And so Jesus responds with *"Right guys ... it is impossible for man, but not with God!" (Verse 27, paraphrased, but accurate!)*

Only by throwing yourself and your priorities on the mercy seat of God can you find salvation! Jesus must become your priority and means to salvation! This is a hard pill to swallow for many, as many people like the idea of salvation but they want it on their terms. They are willing to be *"good people,"* but they want to keep their priorities as they see fit! They may be like this young rich man ... they may come running to see Jesus at church or revival meetings ... but they will not give their all to Christ!

All this of course wakes these guys up, and Peter is the first to speak: *"Lo, we have left all, and have followed you."*

He is looking for some assurance from Jesus at this point ... they are still stunned by all this new understanding! Jesus does affirm their commitment, and then adds that the same commitment level is required by all. Jesus must be a priority for everyone! Lest they misunderstand at this point and think that only poverty will result for those who make Christ a priority, Jesus adds some interesting information in the next few verses.

Jesus says that for those who make Him a priority,

they will yet experience blessings in this life. Jesus says of those who follow Him that they will receive a *"hundred times as much in this present age"* – they will not lack for what is needed in life. *"Houses, family, lands,"* etc. ... we won't be starved or at full loss even in this life; our basic needs will be met and more! BUT – so that a prosperity doctrine isn't read into this, Jesus adds that they will also receive *"persecutions!"* In other words, *life will be filled with both blessing and tough times*, but the final reward is eternal life! This goes to those who keep Him a priority in their lives!

And so, in this context Jesus says that *"the first will be last, and the last first."* Those who put Christ first in their lives will many times by this world be considered last but in eternity they shall be first, and those who put this world first in this life will find out that they are in last place in eternity! – The point: MAKE THE RIGHT PRIORITY NOW!

Luke 9:59-62 gives us Jesus' words:

"He said to another man, 'Follow me.' But he

replied, 'Lord, first let me go and bury my father.' Jesus said to him, 'Let the dead bury their own dead, but you go and proclaim the kingdom of God.' Still another said, 'I will follow you, Lord; but first let me go back and say goodbye to my family.' Jesus replied, 'No one who puts a hand to the plow and looks back is fit for service in the kingdom of God.'"

Here again Jesus is asking for those to *"COME FOLLOW ME."* We are introduced here to a man who Jesus calls to *"come follow me."* Again, we find a man willing to respond to Jesus, in fact this man is ready to follow Jesus. He is not affected by riches like the other man, but he introduces a different kind of priority problem – *procrastination!* This man is not asking to go and bury his father right at the moment; if his dad had just died, he would not have been talking to Jesus. According to Jewish law, the death of a parent required the children to make it an absolute priority to take care of the burial immediately. Even breaking Sabbath laws was acceptable under these circumstances, even breaking other laws, if needed. One did not do anything else but the burial. The fact that this man was on the road talking to Jesus indicates that his dad had not just died. Therefore, his request to *"first go and bury my father"* was really *"let me stay at home, and when my parents are gone, someday I will come and follow you."* This meant some unknown future date since he could not know when his parents would die. In other words, when he was free from other pressing duties he would come and follow Christ someday – he just didn't know when, but someday! At this rate it could be very late in life, and his whole life would prove to have been spent not serving God. Once his home responsibilities were lessened, he would come and follow, at least someday!

Jesus' response almost seems cold, but what He is saying here is to *"let the spiritually dead bury the physically dead,"* implying that *"death"* is a quality they share together! There is a greater life and death, and those who are already dead (spiritually) need life before it is too late! Don't procrastinate and let them die while waiting to take care of a physically dead person! Delay here would be costly to many more people in a way that would be worse than just physical death! Jesus' statement was not a cold response to the need to bury a loved one. He knew this man's heart was to procrastinate following Him and so He was addressing that as the real issue!

Jesus knew this man's real heart issue. If he used this excuse to not make a commitment now, he may later have another excuse!

This man represented the statement of Jesus when he said in Matthew 22:14, *"For many are invited, but few are chosen."* He was putting off and delaying when he would follow Jesus! There are lots of people doing this today, too. This second man was different in that he wasn't seeking a permanent delay like burying a family member, just a reasonable delay that seemed just long enough to say good-bye to his family. Here again is a man that seems willing to follow Jesus, and he makes a reasonable request, but this request hides an issue in his heart that Jesus realizes is blocking his way to Him, and so Jesus challenges it! This man's request demonstrated to Jesus a certain reluctance to make a decision and stick with it. Though this wasn't going to be a long delay like the other man, his reluctance to come right then indicated a pattern that suggested a change of heart later, too!

The man's real problem was in being decisive – or the lack of it. He was reacting reluctantly. If this man was reluctant to obey immediately and wholeheartedly now, he will likely respond this way in the future as well. His test then was to avoid the reluctant nature of his request by not going home to say farewell! Certainly, Jesus is not unreasonable. This request to not go back and say farewell was designed as the test for the real issue of this man's heart, not a doctrine to avoid our loved ones at all cost in following Jesus! This was this man's issue ... he wasn't willing to make a decision when Jesus asked; he was postponing it until later! It was a milder form of procrastination, but a deadly form nonetheless!

Jesus' response to this man's reluctance indicates that Jesus knew this man's reluctance now could be a problem later if allowed to stand, thus He said to him, *"No one who puts his hand to the plow and looks back is fit for service in the kingdom of God."* Lack of decisiveness will cause him to come and go on all kinds of occasions. Jesus' call to follow is not an *"off-on"* game ... it is permanent! This man didn't need big excuses to fall away or to stall; small ones like *"let me just say good-bye to my family"* was all he needed to delay making a decision. If he couldn't choose *"on"* in an easy time, this would prove to be no good when things got tough following Christ!

Jesus' invitation to *"COME FOLLOW ME"* was an immediate one, without delay! *"TODAY IS THE ACCEPTED TIME."* Those who would hesitate now might well do so later, too! While these two men were better than the rich young man who would not change his priorities, they were no better off in the end if they procrastinated in following Jesus. In a sense, they too had their priorities wrong, and the same loss would be felt by all!

How have you responded to Jesus' invitation?

Jesus' invitation to *"come and follow me"* must not be taken lightly! It is not an invitation of convenience, but of total commitment! It is also an invitation that demands an immediate response, not a future response! Following Jesus means not only adventures in glory but also adventures in adversity! This invitation is a working one. How have you responded to Jesus' call to come and follow Him?

Jesus Christ will satisfy the thirsty soul, He IS the water of life and He will give Himself freely to all who are thirsty!

— 4 —

DRINK

MOST OF us take water for granted, at least until we become thirsty! We don't usually think much about water, because we can turn a tap and have all the fresh water in the world. But you realize how important water is when you get really thirsty and can't get a glass of water! Suddenly all you can think about is water! Your whole body craves it, every thought is about it, and your body aches for it!

When we think of the desert, our brain gets pictures of barrenness. Yet, when a rain comes to the desert, all manner of life springs forth even if for just a short time. It can suddenly become a great garden of life when its thirst has been met for a time! Jesus uses this image to make an invitation to all people: *"If anyone is thirsty, let him come to me and drink."*

The Bible teaches us that Jesus Christ will satisfy the thirsty soul, He IS the water of life, and He will give Himself freely to all who are thirsty!

John 4:5-26 tells this story:

"So he came to a town in Samaria called Sychar, near the plot of ground Jacob had given to his son Joseph. Jacob's well was there, and Jesus, tired as he was from the journey, sat down by the well. It was about noon. When a Samaritan woman came to draw water, Jesus said to her, 'Will you give me a drink?' (His disciples had gone into the town to buy food.) The Samaritan woman said to him, 'You are a Jew and I am a Samaritan woman. How can you ask me for a drink?' (For Jews do not associate with Samaritans.)

"Jesus answered her, 'If you knew the gift of God and who it is that asks you for a drink,

you would have asked him and he would have given you living water.' 'Sir,' the woman said, 'you have nothing to draw with and the well is deep. Where can you get this living water? Are you greater than our father Jacob, who gave us the well and drank from it himself, as did also his sons and his livestock?' Jesus answered, 'Everyone who drinks this water will be thirsty again, but whoever drinks the water I give them will never thirst. Indeed, the water I give them will become in them a spring of water welling up to eternal life.'

"The woman said to him, 'Sir, give me this water so that I won't get thirsty and have to keep coming here to draw water.' He told her, 'Go, call your husband and come back.' 'I have no husband,' she replied. Jesus said to her, 'You are right when you say you have no husband. The fact is, you have had five husbands, and the man you now have is not your husband. What you have just said is quite true.' 'Sir,' the woman said, 'I can see that you are a prophet. Our ancestors worshiped on this

mountain, but you Jews claim that the place where we must worship is in Jerusalem.'
'Woman,' Jesus replied, 'believe me, a time is coming when you will worship the Father neither on this mountain nor in Jerusalem. You Samaritans worship what you do not know; we worship what we do know, for salvation is from the Jews. Yet a time is coming and has now come when the true worshipers will worship the Father in the Spirit and in truth, for they are the kind of worshipers the Father seeks. God is spirit, and his worshipers must worship in the Spirit and in truth.'

"The woman said, 'I know that Messiah' (called Christ) 'is coming. When he comes, he will explain everything to us.' Then Jesus declared, 'I, the one speaking to you—I am he.'"

(Paul, in I Corinthians 10:4, gives us this confirmation ... "and [they] drank the same spiritual drink; for they drank from the spiritual rock that accompanied them, and that rock was Christ.")

Here is a woman at a well. Jesus is tired and thirsty and so asks her for a drink. Of course, she is shocked that He would do so, she being a Samaritan and He being a Jew — Jews did not fraternize with Samaritans normally, much less a female one! Jesus of course uses this opportunity to talk to this woman who is living in sin about *"living water"* that He can give her to satisfy her real thirst! Like most people, she assumes He means water from this world. She would be happy not to have to come to this well all the time! She was only thinking about her physical thirst while Jesus was trying to introduce her to a spiritual thirst!

Once she realizes who Jesus is, she gladly partakes of this *"living water,"* and sure enough her joy sends her into the city shouting for people to come and get a drink of *"living water"* themselves! She had been living in the desert for a long time; how wonderful to have her real thirst met — it satisfied so immediately that she dropped her bucket and left it at the well when she ran into town to shout about this new *"living water"* found in Christ! John 4:28 states: *"Then, leaving her water jar, the woman went back to the town and said to the people..."* She had found a source of water greater than physical water! She was so filled that she overflowed, a nice thing to do when in the desert! Once she spread the word, quite a few from the town came out and got a drink as well!

Remember Israel in the desert? They had quite a few problems with water and thirst. Many times they got very thirsty ... and God faithfully sent them water. Paul mentions this as a lesson for us in 1 Corinthians 10:4. Israel all ate the heavenly food and drank the heavenly water that came from a rock, one that Paul says traveled with them, and that rock he calls Christ. Jewish legend says that a rock traveled with Israel throughout the desert and supplied fresh water for them. Paul may be referring to this legend and the fact of that water he identifies as Christ – the source of living water! Here Paul warns however that even though they all partook of the same spiritual benefits, they didn't all find the Promised Land. This was a warning to believers today that we must be careful not to just take those spiritual blessings for granted, to only drink once ... we must continue to drink this *"living water"* daily! Smart people build near water!

Isaiah 44:3 tells us:

"For I will pour water on the thirsty land, and streams on the dry ground; I will pour out my Spirit on your offspring, and my blessing on your descendants."

Isaiah 55:1 says:

"Come, all you who are thirsty, come to the waters; and you who have no money, come, buy and eat! Come, buy wine and milk without money and without cost."

Dryness creates thirst; thirst is a desire. It is clear that many times God allowed Israel's spiritual dryness to take place to provoke a thirst for God again! One of the warnings God had given Israel was about forsaking the covenant with God. If they did the heavens would be shut up and would not give forth rain. This was not just to inflict pain for pain's sake on His people but to remind them of dryness in their soul! The physical was meant to remind them of the spiritual! *It also showed them that material blessings were only appreciated when they first had focused on spiritual things!* Our craving for water can be much greater than our craving for food; we cannot live as long without water as we can without food! To neglect God for even a short time can create a thirsty soul. Dryness destroys life quickly ... look at the deserts; that's how they became so barren – no water, no life! No Christ, no water of life for the soul – just barrenness!

In Isaiah 44:3, God says, *"He will pour water upon him that is thirsty and floods upon dry ground!"* He again offers this invitation in Isaiah 55:1: *"Come, all you who are thirsty, come to the waters..."* To receive, one just has to be thirsty – this is desire! The well is never dry for those who come to God!

John 6:53-66 tells us:

"Jesus said to them, 'Very truly I tell you, unless you eat the flesh of the Son of Man and drink his blood, you have no life in you. Whoever eats my flesh and drinks my blood has eternal life, and I will raise them up at the

last day. For my flesh is real food and my blood is real drink. Whoever eats my flesh and drinks my blood remains in me, and I in them. Just as the living Father sent me and I live because of the Father, so the one who feeds on me will live because of me. This is the bread that came down from heaven. Your ancestors ate manna and died, but whoever feeds on this bread will live forever.' He said this while teaching in the synagogue in Capernaum.

"On hearing it, many of his disciples said, 'This is a hard teaching. Who can accept it?'

"Aware that his disciples were grumbling about this, Jesus said to them, 'Does this offend you? Then what if you see the Son of Man ascend to where he was before! The Spirit gives life; the flesh counts for nothing. The words I have spoken to you—they are full of the Spirit and life. Yet there are some of you who do not believe.' For Jesus had known from the beginning which of them did not believe and who would betray him. He went on to say,

'This is why I told you that no one can come to me unless the Father has enabled them.'

"From this time many of his disciples turned back and no longer followed him."

John 7:37-39 goes on to say:

"On the last and greatest day of the festival, Jesus stood and said in a loud voice, 'Let anyone who is thirsty come to me and drink. Whoever believes in me, as Scripture has said, rivers of living water will flow from within them.' By this he meant the Spirit, whom those who believed in him were later to receive. Up to that time the Spirit had not been given, since Jesus had not yet been glorified."

Jesus explains to the crowd that in order for them to know life in Him they would have to *"eat His flesh and drink his blood!"* They could hardly believe their ears! Jesus seemed to be talking about cannibalism! The idea of eating His flesh and drinking His blood seemed crazy, but of course Jesus wasn't talking about actually eating His flesh and literally drinking His blood. He was talking about His sacrifice on the cross and accepting it. This is the whole concept of communion today. The bread represents His broken body, and the blood represents the new life we have in Him through His shed blood on Calvary! Jesus makes the offer in no uncertain terms: there can be no life for them if they don't eat and drink Him — if they don't receive Him as their supply!

This was a tough call, and indeed in verse 66 it states that after Jesus explained the meaning of this call, many lost interest in Him. *"After this hard saying, many of his disciples no longer followed him!"* They were not that hungry or that thirsty! And so, they turned away from the only source of life they could have known! They decided to settle for physical bread and water rather than satisfy their soul's spiritual hunger and thirst! Their thirst was not great enough and so they remained barren and dead!

It would be rare indeed to find a disciple that has absolutely no thirst for God! They might be a disciple when things are good, but as soon as things get tough or commitment is called for, they drift aside if their thirst is not strong enough! Only the really thirsty keep seeking for something to drink! This call by Jesus to be committed, to be so thirsty for Him that all else is nothing in comparison, was too tough for some to hear ... and so they left following Jesus.

How about you? How thirsty are you really? When the call for real commitment comes, do you run?

This was the last day of the FEAST OF TABERNACLES, celebrating the time Israel lived in the desert. Traditionally, on the last day, water from the pool of Siloam was offered up as part of the closing ceremonies. It was here and likely at this moment that Jesus stood and made an offer to satisfy a thirst with living water that was better than water from the pool of Siloam! The waters from Siloam were the waters people bathed in for healing; they were waters thought to have special properties ... BUT Jesus offers them better water – living healing water, HIM! Jesus stands and makes His offer, *"If anyone is thirsty, let him come to me and drink."* If they thought these few vessels of water from the pool of Siloam could be helpful, they hadn't seen the flood of water from Jesus that could meet all their needs! Jesus then adds, *"Whoever believes in me as the Scripture has said, streams of living water will flow from within him!"*

Jesus offers more than a trickle! He offers a flood!

Jesus is promising here that for those who are thirsty, they not only will be refreshed, they will be overflowing with streams of living water. This is a promise of the Holy Spirit that was to come through Christ's death and resurrection. No longer would the soul of man need to be thirsty! Jesus would open the floodgates of Heaven and pour out His Spirit to those who asked!

Have you taken the plunge? Are you thirsty? He will satisfy! *"COME AND DRINK!"*

Thirst is a powerful drive! Physical thirst cannot match, however, the powerful thirst of the soul! We are born thirsty, and while we have many different sources to "drink" from, there is only one that satisfies the heart, the LIVING WATERS OF JESUS! The invitation by Christ still stands today: "*If anyone is thirsty, let him come to me and drink.*" Even in the desert you can have a full supply! Has your thirst been met?

Jesus, knowing their need for restoration and encouragement reaches out to them and invites them to "COME AND DINE," to enjoy His fellowship and His provisions.

— 5 —

DINE

HAVE YOU ever had a rough day or even a rough week — and you have failed miserably on the job or even at home? You come home and feel tired and weak; you are not exactly good company. At such times you get a phone call and a friend invites you to a meal to relax and refresh yourself. It can be so wonderful!

This is what the Lord does in this invitation ... it is just after the crucifixion of Jesus. The disciples are battling discouragement, and some like Peter have horrible feelings of failure they haven't fully dealt with yet. They have pulled back spiritually, with feelings of personal failure and even a group failure with shattered dreams and expectations.

Peter denied Jesus three times. The rest ran away from the cross, except John. Judas committed suicide, nothing worked out like they had expected, and no great kingdom came. They felt discouraged and weak, like failures, and they were probably fostering anger and doubts.

In the midst of this, Jesus appears and offers an invitation: *"Come and dine"* (John 21:12, KJV). The Bible teaches us that Jesus offers us a place of refreshing when we have failed or are fearful, His love is so great for us that He seeks to renew us. All we have to do is accept the invitation!

John 21:1-3 paints the event:

> *"Afterward Jesus appeared again to his disciples, by the Sea of Galilee. It happened this way: Simon Peter, Thomas (also known as Didymus), Nathanael from Cana in Galilee, the sons of Zebedee, and two other disciples were together. 'I'm going out to fish,' Simon*

Peter told them, and they said, 'We'll go with you.' So they went out and got into the boat, but that night they caught nothing."

We are introduced to a ragtag group of seven men who are totally discouraged and feeling aimless. Their hopes and dreams are dashed; they are uncertain as to what has recently happened to them. They couldn't come up with answers for all the horrible things that had taken place, and even if they did have any ideas, they were dealing with their own feelings of failure and running away from Jesus. There was lots of guilt in their midst! This becomes evident in Peter's statement in verse 3: *"I'm going out to fish!"* It is stated very matter of fact, as though there is nothing else to do – or nothing else he wants to do! An expanded version of this verse expresses it this way: *"I'm going off, breaking my former connections (kingdom work stuff), to apply myself to my former fishing business."* He was turning back to his old occupation, trying to forget the years spent working for the Kingdom of God – he felt he had failed horribly. The rest of the men agree to go along to fish with him. They had nothing better to do either!

Together they go and experience even more failure! They catch nothing all night! Things were not at all like they expected them to be in the Kingdom of God. They weren't going to put all their eggs in that basket again, but now they couldn't even catch fish like they used to! Their level of trust in what they believed was in serious disrepair!

John 21:4-5 is the moment when help arrives:

"Early in the morning, Jesus stood on the shore, but the disciples did not realize that it was Jesus. He called out to them, 'Friends, haven't you any fish?' 'No,' they answered."

Though they were in a defeated attitude, Jesus sees their need and comes to meet them! The Lord knows when we have failed, and He is concerned about how we are doing! They needed restoration, so Jesus makes an appearance to minister to them! Their present failure to catch fish however only added to their sense of previous failure so that they didn't even notice it was Jesus. They weren't even looking anymore for the Lord!

They couldn't even see Jesus when He was standing right in front of them! They were only looking at their own sense of failure and disappointments! They were too focused on their own failures and loss of dreams to even notice it was Jesus who had come to refresh them!

Failure can hold us in a grip that can distort our whole perspective about God and others ... even ourselves! Jesus wasn't through with them. Thank God He doesn't just cast us away every time we fail! They needed a visit from the Lord even when they didn't recognize it was the Lord! They were just drifting and failing – it was time to get them back on course!

John 21:6-9 reveals the revelation:

"He said, 'Throw your net on the right side of the boat and you will find some.' When they did, they were unable to haul the net in because of the large number of fish. Then the disciple whom Jesus loved said to Peter, 'It is the Lord!' As soon as Simon Peter heard him say, 'It is

the Lord,' he wrapped his outer garment around him (for he had taken it off) and jumped into the water. The other disciples followed in the boat, towing the net full of fish, for they were not far from shore, about a hundred yards. When they landed, they saw a fire of burning coals there with fish on it, and some bread."

In their minds they must have assumed they had lost favor with Jesus, so it was back to their previous occupation! However, Jesus loves us more than we give Him credit for. It is hard to lose the favor of God! *Rather than send a storm to sink their ship and drown them for the way they had abandoned Him during the crucifixion, He instead sits down and prepares for them a relaxing refreshing meal, a time of fellowship with just them!* Jesus loves these men and nothing was more important than restoring them! And, this is true with us, too! Notice Jesus' greeting to them: *"Friends, haven't you any fish?"* (Note: in the Greek this question was put by Jesus in a way that reveals He already knew the answer: *"Friends, you haven't caught any fish, have you?"* Jesus addresses them AS FRIENDS,

He loves them and has come to restore them!)

Jesus gives them a familiar incident to open their eyes to who He was. He asks them to cast their nets on the *"right"* side of the boat *(the starboard side)*. As they obey Jesus, they suddenly find a huge catch of fish! Funny, but this had happened before in their lives when they had listened to Jesus — yes — it must be Him! This opened John's eyes first, and he is the first to recognize that this was no ordinary man on shore. It had to be Jesus! He turns and tells Peter this ... and Peter turns and puts on his clothes and jumps into the water! Peter does not walk on water this time; he swims with his clothes on! It was considered a sacred thing to greet another person; this could not be done without being properly dressed!

Peter drops everything to get to Jesus. A new flash of hope of renewed desire to be right with Jesus bursts in his soul again! On shore, Jesus has already prepared a hot meal, a warm setting, and an opportunity for fellowship! Jesus needs nothing, but He desires their fellowship!

John 21:10-14 is a time of renewed faith:

> *"Jesus said to them, 'Bring some of the fish you have just caught.' So Simon Peter climbed back into the boat and dragged the net ashore. It was full of large fish, 153, but even with so many the net was not torn. Jesus said to them, 'Come and have breakfast.' None of the disciples dared ask him, 'Who are you?' They knew it was the Lord. Jesus came, took the bread and gave it to them, and did the same with the fish. This was now the third time Jesus appeared to his disciples after he was raised from the dead."*

Jesus invites them to bring some of the fish they had just caught, although He didn't need them – perhaps He felt they needed to feel they could contribute something, too! Jesus is concerned about their way of seeing themselves. They saw only their failure, their defeat. He would now change this. Like us, so many times when we fail, it is hard to come close again to the Lord, because we are overwhelmed by our failure!

We do this all the time. We miss the bigger picture for the smaller failures that consume our minds! Jesus invites them to *"come and dine,"* to come and sit and break their fast, or to have breakfast with Him — to enjoy fellowship with God! What a statement: God still wants fellowship with us even when we fail Him! He hands them bread and meat ... much the same way He had always done! He desired to heal their hurt and restore their mission and thinking, and especially their relationship to Him! He was concerned about them!

Jesus knew where to find them, how to get to them, how to heal them, how to encourage them!

John 21:15-19 offers healing to Peter:

"When they had finished eating, Jesus said to Simon Peter, 'Simon son of John, do you love me more than these?' 'Yes, Lord,' he said, 'you know that I love you.' Jesus said, 'Feed my lambs.'

"Again Jesus said, 'Simon son of John, do you

love me?' He answered, 'Yes, Lord, you know that I love you.' Jesus said, 'Take care of my sheep.'

"The third time he said to him, 'Simon son of John, do you love me?' Peter was hurt because Jesus asked him the third time, 'Do you love me?' He said, 'Lord, you know all things; you know that I love you.' Jesus said, 'Feed my sheep. Very truly I tell you, when you were younger you dressed yourself and went where you wanted; but when you are old you will stretch out your hands, and someone else will dress you and lead you where you do not want to go.' Jesus said this to indicate the kind of death by which Peter would glorify God. Then he said to him, 'Follow me!'"

Jesus is not only interested in them as a group. He also knew one of them needed some personal attention ... Peter! Jesus begins with Peter by asking an odd and interesting question: *"Simon, son of John, do you truly love me more than these?"* This must have grabbed Peter's attention, first, because Jesus doesn't call him *"Peter,"* but calls him by his old name *"Simon,"* and second, it was Peter who had earlier claimed a superior love for Jesus than the other disciples (See Mark 14:29 where Peter said that even if all the others deserted Jesus, he wouldn't; he claimed to love Him better than they did!). This was the point of Peter beginning to fail, and this is where Jesus would start to bring healing!

The point of all this was to deal with Peter's failure, not by ignoring it, but by dealing directly with it!

Peter is quick to respond that yes indeed he loves the Lord, for which Jesus then adds, *"FEED my lambs." Jesus responds by letting Peter know He wants him back in ministry, serving!* The call here was to *"feed"* the lambs ... in other words, give good food to the newborn babes, the work of the Shepherd! Jesus again asks a second time about Peter's love and again Peter, being grieved, says of course he loves the Lord! Peter was now hurt that Jesus had questioned him twice. Jesus wanted to get Peter to deal with his feelings and affirm his love an equal number of times for the number of times he had denied Jesus, to heal each one of Peter's earlier denials, and this was #2! Jesus adds, *"Take care of my sheep,"*... a reference to the older sheep in a fold, using the term *"tend"* or *"take care"* ... meaning to guide and even discipline ... again the work of a Shepherd!

A third time Jesus questions him about his love, and the final denial is dealt with by a third affirmation by Peter. Jesus adds this time to *"feed my sheep,"* now including the entire fold, young and old and all between!

This was the work of ministry; Jesus had not given up on Peter! The call to the cross was for Peter as well, and it was not going to be an easy cross to bear. It would take deep love for the Lord to endure the cross he would have to bear! Being a follower of Jesus is not an easy task, it is not just another thing to do, and it is not a cheap cross!

Jesus was both healing old wounds in Peter and also letting him know that ministry needed deep love! Only Peter's deep love for Jesus could keep their friendship strong enough for Peter to make it in ministry.

This nice fellowship on the lakeshore, however, was intended as more than just a time of friendship. It was also preparation and dedication to a job yet to be done!

John 21:19-23 redirects Peter once more:

"Jesus said this to indicate the kind of death by which Peter would glorify God. Then he said to him, 'Follow me!' Peter turned and saw that the disciple whom Jesus loved was following them. (This was the one who had leaned back against Jesus at the supper and had said, 'Lord, who is going to betray you?') When Peter saw him, he asked, 'Lord, what about him?' Jesus answered, 'If I want him to remain alive until I return, what is that to you? You must follow me.' Because of this, the rumor spread among the believers that this disciple would not die. But Jesus did not say that he would not die; he only said, 'If I want

him to remain alive until I return, what is that to you?'"

Peter was doing well until then, when he came upon an old habit – looking at others! Jesus' last words to Peter mirror the first words He spoke to Peter: *"FOLLOW ME!"* Peter however turns and looks at John and asks what is going to happen to John! Jesus has to remind Peter to quit worrying about John and to worry about Peter! Again Jesus adds, *"You must follow me!"* ... get your eyes off of what I am doing with John and keep them on me! If Peter didn't, ministry would become impossible; he would be too prone to being either smug or disappointed with God if he kept his eyes on what God was doing with others and compared himself to them! This has always been the downfall and struggle with many Christians ... we are supposed to be following Jesus and not others!

Now they were all restored to fellowship, Peter's failures had been healed, new direction given, the right focus was in place, and the work of God took off! All because a bunch of discouraged guys accepted an invitation from God to *"COME AND DINE!"*

Do you need to accept God's invitation to renew your fellowship? Have you been refreshed by God's provisions? Do you have clear insight into what He is calling you to do?

IF NOT ... *"COME AND DINE!"*

This invitation by Jesus was to a group of disheartened and failing disciples! Jesus, knowing their need for restoration and encouragement, reaches out to them and invites them to *"COME AND DINE,"* to enjoy His fellowship and His provisions. This invitation is for the weary and the struggling disciple, for the one who is struggling with failures and can't get past them. For those who come, they will find fellowship with God and healing! *"COME AND DINE!"*

We will be receiving a great inheritance from our Lord, one we are invited to come and take!

— 6 —

INHERIT

WE WILL soon reach the time of the year when children begin looking forward to a very special holiday ... Christmas is coming! We often find that the closer we get to a special day, whether a birthday, a vacation, or a visit to Grandma's house, we find ourselves getting more and more excited. Holidays usually involve time off, good fellowship, sometimes presents, etc. They help us endure the hard times and the everyday hectic schedules we keep. We keep saying, *"In a few more weeks I'll get several days off and some well-deserved rest and have some fun."*

When we examine the events of this world, we know that we are getting closer to the coming of the

Lord, a really special day! We will be receiving a great inheritance from our Lord, one we are invited to come and take! Like a special day that is coming, the closer it gets, the more anticipation and excitement we experience — if we are ready for it!

The Bible has put great emphasis on Christ's second coming ... there are over 1,800 references in the Old Testament alone on the return of the Messiah. In the New Testament there is no less than one in every thirty verses about the second coming of Christ! For every prophecy in the Bible about Jesus' first coming, there are eight about His second coming! So, if the first proved reliable, be sure the second will be also! The Bible teaches us that we are invited to enjoy a great inheritance in Christ. Our future is bright and His invitation is clear, *"Come ... and inherit!"*

Matthew 25:31 tells us:

"When the Son of Man comes in his glory, and all the angels with him, he will sit on his glorious throne."

While Jesus' first coming had to do with coming as a servant, humble; this second coming will be with glory and power as King ... and all the angels with Him. Jesus' first coming was to be the Savior. His second coming will be as the judge of all mankind! This is the picture here of Him sitting on a throne. Surrounded by His angels, He will judge all. This judgment will have nothing to do with the legal system of this world. The rich and famous won't have their high-priced lawyers to help them.

How very different is Jesus ... He comes for those who will come to Him, and to them He offers a great inheritance not based on wealth or power on earth. His call is based on our relationship with Him – He opens up the barriers; this can't be done by anything on this earth!

Matthew 16:27 reveals His glory:

"For the Son of Man is going to come in his Father's glory with his angels, and then he will reward each person according to what they

have done."

Matthew 25:32-33 reveals His purpose:

"All the nations will be gathered before him, and he will separate the people one from another as a shepherd separates the sheep from the goats. He will put the sheep on his right and the goats on his left."

The purpose of Jesus' coming is made clear here. It is to judge the people and nations of the world. Here all mankind will be gathered before God's great judgment throne. The purpose of this time is to separate the people of the world into two groups, and only two groups – there is no middle ground! Most people don't even want to think of the future, but this coming separation will be real!

This time will be real and forever; God will divide the masses of humanity, past, present, and future into two groups! It is vitally important who you listen to while in this life, for it will make the difference for all eternity!!!

For believers this time is going to be one of great joy, but for the lost it will be the greatest sorrow in all eternity! Verse 33 makes it quite clear that there is a final separation. No universalism can be taught here!! As real as Heaven is, so is Hell!

Matthew 25:34-40 reveals His favor:

"Then the King will say to those on his right, 'Come, you who are blessed by my Father; take your inheritance, the kingdom prepared for you since the creation of the world. For I was hungry and you gave me something to eat, I was thirsty and you gave me something to drink, I was a stranger and you invited me in, I needed clothes and you clothed me, I was sick and you looked after me, I was in prison and you came to visit me.'

"Then the righteous will answer him, 'Lord, when did we see you hungry and feed you, or thirsty and give you something to drink? When did we see you a stranger and invite you

in, or needing clothes and clothe you? When did we see you sick or in prison and go to visit you?'

"The King will reply, 'Truly I tell you, whatever you did for one of the least of these brothers and sisters of mine, you did for me.'"

The favored placement by monarchs in ancient times was to be put on their right side ... here Jesus separates the sheep and puts them on His right side! Jesus also states clearly that this inheritance was prepared for His sheep from the very foundation of the Earth! God's plan has always included salvation! The life we live now has impact on the future life we will live!

The Lord goes on to explain why they were honored to receive this inheritance: There was evidence in their lifetime of the Spirit's work in their hearts. In fact, this passage clearly indicates that when the Lord lives in a heart, there is always clear and real evidence! It is also clear that they weren't doing all these wonderful things to just get a reward, for they are startled by the fact that Jesus praises them!

They lived this way because Christ was in their hearts and not just to earn Heaven!

The point Jesus is making is quite clear, their lives reflected the change of heart Jesus had brought them. They served without attempting to earn their salvation, for they were quite surprised when Jesus praised them for their labors and work! They did what came natural from their supernatural change of heart. Their life reflected the character of Christ in action! Any and all revivals do this: people become servants, the love of Christ in their life becomes more evident and they do it without manipulating God. They do it because of God's love in their hearts!

Too many people think that getting saved means they should do great things for God, and for some they won't serve unless it is something big.

Jesus praises His sheep for their lifestyle, their ministry to the weak as well as the strong, for every time they served others, they were in fact serving Him!

This would not go unrewarded! The righteous have hard and real evidence to their changed nature! Jesus earlier had stated, *"By their fruit you shall know them."* Those now separated to His right are invited to *"take your inheritance."* God has prepared a place in Heaven for those who are His, not just those who say they are His — but those who show they are! What a praise this is, Heaven is a real hope and eternal life with Christ is a real future for the real saints!

Matthew 25:41-46 reveals His wrath:

"Then he will say to those on his left, 'Depart from me, you who are cursed, into the eternal fire prepared for the devil and his angels. For I was hungry and you gave me nothing to eat, I was thirsty and you gave me nothing to drink, I was a stranger and you did not invite me in, I needed clothes and you did not clothe me, I was sick and in prison and you did not look after me.'

"They also will answer, 'Lord, when did we see you hungry or thirsty or a stranger or needing

clothes or sick or in prison, and did not help you?'

"He will reply, 'Truly I tell you, whatever you did not do for one of the least of these, you did not do for me.'

"Then they will go away to eternal punishment, but the righteous to eternal life."

Now Jesus does the same thing with the other group on his left, the *"goats!"* Here again Jesus points to their lifetime actions! They all fall short of showing Christ's nature in their lives. Jesus runs down the same list only showing how they DIDN'T DO THESE THINGS! How well will you do one day when Jesus asks these questions about you? It is interesting to note that Jesus describes *"Hell"* as the place designed for the *"Devil and his angels."* Hell was never intended to hold human beings; sin separates us from God, and since there are only two dwelling places in eternity, and you miss Heaven by living in sin, you send yourself to the only other place ... Hell! It is really more a matter of INHERITING HELL if you reject

Heaven! Jesus here throws an interesting twist to the concept of SIN. He explains here that SIN is not just WHAT WE DO ... IT CAN ALSO BE WHAT WE DON'T DO! These are the sins of omission! It is stated this way in JAMES 4:17 (KJV): *"Therefore to him that knoweth to do good, and doeth it not, to him it is sin!"* Jesus seems to be equating here that the sins of omission are greater than the sins of commission! Why? Because they rob others of the opportunity to see Christ in action!

Notice the response of the wicked: with injured innocence they ask, *"Lord, when did we see you ..."* They plead ignorance of Jesus' needs! They fail to see the obvious; they lived for themselves, the very nature of all sin! Their excuses however do not stand; they had lived their lives for only self, now they would get exactly what they lived for – ONLY SELF – a place called Hell where God won't bother them, or anyone else. They will live in self-exiled darkness forever. Jesus in no way waters down the concept of Hell here; it is real and will be the final destination of those who reject Christ and who live their lives for self. The sin of doing nothing is as damaging as the sins of doing wrong! They too leave others in darkness. Jesus' invitation still stands today; take it while you can!

You can choose to come and inherit Christ's salvation and reward; it's your call NOW.

Jesus' greatest invitation to us still stands as an open door, to *"come ... and inherit."* This invitation is to an event yet to come, the invitation has gone out, and we yet await the event! In this invitation, however, two possible outcomes are waiting; and the choice of which one is deeply affected by our actions now! Like all inheritances, the quality of it depends on the investments and management taken during an entire lifetime. Have you invested wisely? How much are you putting in your retirement account?!

About Tim R. Barker

Reverend Tim R. Barker is the Superintendent of the South Texas District of the Assemblies of God which is headquartered in Houston, Texas

He is a graduate of Southwestern Assemblies of God University, with a Bachelor of Science degree in General Ministries/Biblical Studies, with a minor in music. He also received a Master of Arts in Practical Theology from SAGU and received his Doctorate of Ministry Degree from West Coast Seminary.

Reverend Barker was ordained by the Assemblies of God in 1989. He began his ministry in the South Texas District in 1984 as youth & music minister and continued his ministry as Pastor, Executive Presbyter (2006 – 2009) and Executive Secretary-Treasurer (2009 – 2011) in the South Texas District, where he served until his election as the South Texas District Superintendent in 2011.

By virtue of his district office, Reverend Barker is a member of the District's Executive Presbytery and the General Presbytery of the General Council of the Assemblies of God, Springfield, Missouri. He is a member of the Executive Board of Regents for Southwestern Assemblies of God University, Waxahachie, Texas, and SAGU-American Indian College, Phoenix, Arizona. He is a member of the Board of Directors of Pleasant Hills Children's Home, Fairfield, Texas, as well as numerous other boards and committees.

Reverend Barker and his wife, Jill, married in 1983, have been blessed with two daughters. Jordin and her husband, Stancle Williams, who serves as the South Texas District Youth Director. Abrielle and her husband, Nolan McLaughlin are church planters of Motion Church in San Antonio. The Barkers have five grandchildren, Braylen, Emory and Landon Williams and Kingston and London McLaughlin.

His unique style of pulpit ministry and musical background challenges the body of Christ, with an appeal that reaches the generations.

A Final Word

You can find Tim on the South Texas District website at www.stxag.org, on Facebook, or at his Houston office when he's not traveling his home state ministering in the churches across the South Texas District.

He'd be thrilled to connect with you and share stories of God's faithfulness.

Additional Books by
Tim R. Barker

If you liked this book, you may be interested in additional books Tim has written. Turn the page for short descriptions of each book. All are available on Amazon.

My *Jesus* Journey

This soul-building, introspective 4-book series reveals Tim's innermost heart on subjects that affect all of us, from Cooperation to Loyalty to The Truth of Salvation and more.

The books in this series include:

My Jesus Journey
My Jesus Journey: Crescendo
My Jesus Journey: Glissando
My Jesus Journey: Rhapsody

At *Your* Feet

In this book, you will read of God's favor and His redemption, for you are chosen and forgiven. In Jesus, you can find the rest you desire, for at His feet, His joy becomes whole.

Come to Jesus today. He holds His hand out to you.

The Lord with Us
from the Book of Hebrews

Do you have a relationship with Jesus? The rewards are great, but if we fail to heed the warnings in the Word, the consequences are also great.

Even if we call ourselves Christian, we must live according to God's will. The Lord is with us when we walk with Him. This is the message from the book of Hebrews.

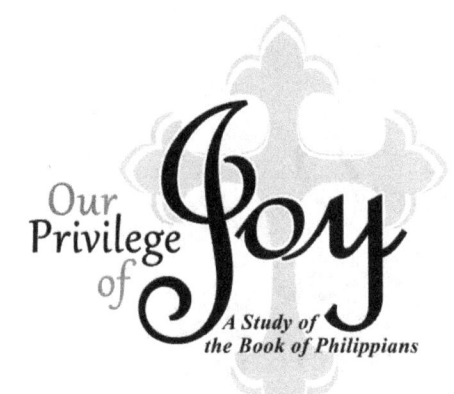

Our Privilege of Joy
A Study of the Book of Philippians

Philippians is our blueprint from the Father, our plan for joy. It was written by the hand of Paul during his time in a Roman prison, but the voice is the Father's, entreating us to lift our hands in praise to Him, and to find joy even in the difficult parts of our lives.

NAMES OF GOD

Our name tells people who we are.

What about the name Christian? That's what the followers of Jesus call themselves. What information can people glean about us when we put a fish symbol on the bumper of our car, or we wear a cross around our neck? And, importantly, do our actions live up to their expectations?

This book is an in-depth teaching about the ten names of God.

The Vision of Nehemiah
God's Plan for Righteous Living

The Book of Nehemiah reveals a vital truth that our instant society often overlooks. Determination can take us only so far in achieving the goals God has for today's Church.

Winning the lost for Christ takes preparation in both our time and our finances. We become the "right stuff" for achieving God's plan when we are willing to risk everything for Him.

God's Revelation and Your Future

The book of Revelation is first and foremost a revelation about Jesus, not just the future.

John reveals Christ as the King of Glory, the conqueror, the one in charge of history, the one who alone controls the future, controls the nations, controls all the universe! This is the Jesus who is coming!

The book of Revelation shows us the glorified Christ and the certainty of His ruling over all things. We are not stumbling toward an uncertain future, but we must be in fellowship with the King!

Truth, Love & Redemption

The Holy Spirit For Today

There is no greater empowerment for the Christian of today than to seek out the Holy Spirit. It was considered vital in the early days of Christendom. Now, many times it is pushed aside as "for then" and not "for now."

We are in greater need of the truth, love, and redemption that flows from an encounter with the Holy Spirit than ever before. The Scriptures tell us that our realization of our need for Christ flows from the Spirit. Even before we accept Christ, the Holy Spirit draws us to Him.

The Call of Ephesians
Building the Church of Today

Paul understood that legalism can become a hindrance to our Christian walk and that we must focus on Christ and Christ alone. When our faith hits the road, God is there with us. He challenges us to trust Him to walk at our side through every challenge we might face.

When we do, we become mighty warriors in God's army.

That's Paul's message in a nutshell, and it's vital we take it to heart.

The Twelve
Taking up the Mantle of Christ

Twelve men were chosen to fulfill Christ's legacy on the earth.

Eleven looked to Jesus for the answers to life's questions. One chose the world and the world failed him.

These men were as varied as the members of our modern church, at times at odds with one another, but forged by Jesus into a single unit that overcame everything the devil could throw at them. What lesson can we learn from them?

Our only option is to choose Christ.

End Times

Scripture provides us a timeline of events that signal that the end is coming soon.

1. The Church Age
2. The Rapture of the Church
3. The Tribulation
4. The Second Coming of Jesus Christ
5. The Millennium
6. The Great White Throne Judgment
7. New Heavens and New Earth

Follow along through each of these Biblical timeline events.

Anticipating the Return of Christ

Are we waiting or are we watching for His appearance in the skies? The difference is in being ready for His return and risking missing Him altogether.

This book covers six areas of preparation for the Return of Christ.

1. Waiting
2. Mindful
3. Joyful
4. Praying
5. Thanking
6. Faithful.

Are you anticipating Christ's return? I am.

Made in United States
Orlando, FL
26 July 2022